Colin
Powell

Catherine Reef

Twenty-First Century Books

A Division of Henry Holt and Co., Inc.
Frederick, Maryland

Published by
Twenty-First Century Books
A Division of Henry Holt and Co., Inc.
38 South Market Street
Frederick, Maryland 21701

Text Copyright © 1992
Catherine Reef

Printed in Mexico
10 9 8 7 6 5 4 3 2 1

Library of Congress Cataloging in Publication Data
Reef, Catherine
Colin Powell
(An African-American Soldiers Book)
Includes bibliographical references and index.
Summary: Traces the life and career of the Army general who
was appointed National Security Adviser by Ronald Reagan and
became the country's first black chairman of the Joint Chiefs of
Staff in 1989.
1. Powell, Colin L., 1937- —Juvenile literature. 2. Generals—
United States—Biography—Juvenile literature. 3. Afro-American
generals—Biography—Juvenile literature. 4. United States. Army—
Biography—Juvenile literature. [1. Powell, Colin L. 2. Generals.
3. Afro-Americans—Biography.] I. Title. II. Series: African-
American Soldiers.
E840.5.P68R44 1992 355'.0092—dc20 [B] 91-45129 CIP AC
ISBN 0-8050-2136-1

PHOTO CREDITS

cover: flag by Fred P. Eckert/FPG
International; portrait courtesy of
the Department of Defense.
3: Bettmann. **4:** UPI/Bettmann.
9: Department of Defense.
12: UPI/Bettmann. **15:** courtesy
of the Office of the Joint Chiefs
of Staff. **17:** courtesy of the
Office of the Joint Chiefs of
Staff. **18:** AP/Wide World
Photos. **19:** courtesy of the
Office of the Joint Chiefs of
Staff. **23:** Bettmann. **25:** National
Archives. **26:** National Archives.
28: Leonard Freed/Magnum
Photos. **33:** Charles Moore/Black
Star. **34:** Bob Adelman/Magnum
Photos. **36:** UPI/Bettmann.
38: UPI/Bettmann. **39:** courtesy
of the Office of the Joint Chiefs
of Staff. **40:** UPI/Bettmann.
45: courtesy of the Office of the
Joint Chiefs of Staff. **48:** AP/Wide
World Photos. **53:** UPI/Bettmann.
55: AP/Wide World Photos.
58-59: Department of Defense.
60: AP/Wide World Photos.
61: Margaret Thomas/The
Washington Post. **63:** Reuters/
Bettmann. **65:** Department of
Defense. **66:** Reuters/Bettmann.
70: Reuters/Bettmann.
73: Chester Higgins, Jr./
NYT Pictures.

Contents

Chapter 1

A Tradition
of Service

The invasion came while most people slept. On August 2, 1990, tanks from Iraq drove across the dark desert into the nation of Kuwait. Long lines of Iraqi troops marched across the border. Above their heads, helicopters and fighter jets filled the starry sky.

Saddam Hussein, the Iraqi leader, had ordered his best soldiers to take over Kuwait, one of his Middle East neighbors. By dawn, hundreds of Iraqi tanks had rolled into the nation's capital, Kuwait City. Thousands of Iraqi soldiers had positioned themselves at key places across Kuwait, and others had moved on to the border with Saudi Arabia.

At his home in Virginia, General Colin Powell first heard the news by telephone. Throughout the night, the general stayed close to the phone. His staff at the Pentagon, the headquarters of the U.S.

In 1989, Colin Powell became chairman of the Joint Chiefs of Staff.

Defense Department, called him as soon as any information from the Middle East arrived.

Before most Americans got out of bed the next morning, General Colin Powell was already hard at work. As chairman of the Joint Chiefs of Staff, Powell holds the highest military position in the nation. The group of military officers headed by Colin Powell is responsible for preparing America's defense strategy and for supervising the conduct of military operations.

Powell knew that George Bush, the president of the United States, would soon be turning to him for advice. He intended to be prepared.

Colin Powell had been surprised by the Iraqi invasion. Hussein's huge army had not appeared ready to attack. But Powell was determined not to be surprised again.

Hours after the invasion, General Powell met with General H. Norman Schwarzkopf, commander of the American forces in the Middle East. He also listened to the opinions of the National Security Council, a group of high-level advisers to the president. The president's military and civilian advisers sounded the same ominous note. This was not a minor dispute between two faraway countries. The invasion of Kuwait was a serious threat to Saudi

Arabia and other countries. It seemed to Powell that the United States had to act right away.

"Draw a line in the sand," Powell advised the president. He urged Bush to send a large military force to the Middle East—and to do so quickly. General Powell wanted Saddam Hussein to realize what would happen if he crossed the Saudi Arabian border—the "line in the sand." The Iraqi leader needed to know, Powell said, "that if he attacks Saudi Arabia, he attacks the United States."

Colin Powell's real goal in sending troops to the Persian Gulf, however, was not war, but peace. A strong display of American military strength, he hoped, would prove to Hussein that another attack could not succeed.

A tall, solid man whose dark hair is touched with gray, Powell calmly awaited the president's orders. A soldier for more than 30 years, he had seen America at war before. And he knew that wars are not fought by tanks and planes and ships. They are fought by men and women—people it was his job to lead and protect.

Yet when President Bush ordered thousands of American soldiers to Saudi Arabia, Powell carried out the order with confidence. He was certain that these men and women had received the best training possible. They could be depended on to do their job well. "Confidence comes from thorough preparation," Powell said. "It's something I learned over the years."

Thirty years of military service had thoroughly prepared Powell for both war and peace. He entered the Army in 1958. In 1962, he traveled to South Vietnam, where he served as a military adviser to the army of that Asian nation. Powell returned to Vietnam in 1968. He and other Americans fought alongside South Vietnamese soldiers.

Colin Powell has commanded troops in Germany, Korea, and the United States. In 1987, he was appointed President Ronald Reagan's national security adviser. In that position, he counseled the president on how to protect the United States from foreign threats. Colin Powell was the nation's first African-American national security adviser, and in 1989, he became the first black chairman of the Joint Chiefs of Staff. In 1991, he was appointed to a second term as chairman.

For Colin Powell, success means simply being a good soldier, doing his best for his country. "I don't sit around and say, 'Gee, I'm the most powerful black man in the country,' " he said. "I just try to do my job."

Doing that job has meant facing tough challenges and making tough decisions. Less than three months after he was named chairman of the Joint Chiefs, Colin Powell recommended that American troops be sent to Panama. Only eight months later, he began to plan Operation Desert Shield—the campaign to defend Saudi Arabia if Iraq attacked.

When war did occur in the Middle East, in January 1991, many Americans followed the events on television. They saw Powell explain the war in special news reports. His calm, confident manner helped to ease the fears of a worried nation.

General Colin Powell follows a long tradition of African-American service in the U.S. military. It is a heritage that he often remembers. "It was

Powell works with other members of the Joint Chiefs of Staff to prepare the nation's defense strategy.

on this road to the future, paved with the blood and sacrifice of black Americans, that I became the first black chairman of the Joint Chiefs of Staff," he said.

Black soldiers have fought in each of America's wars, and each time these soldiers have had to overcome prejudice and prove their worthiness to fight. "I climbed on the backs of the great black men and women," Colin Powell stated, "and I never ever forget where I came from."

Today, Powell strives to set an example for young African Americans. "I am mindful that the struggle is not over," he says. The struggle will not end, Colin Powell believes, "until every American is able to find his or her own place in our society, limited only by his or her own ability and his or her own dream."

But Colin Powell also believes that even with equal opportunities, young Americans will have to work hard if they want to achieve success. "You must be ready for opportunity when it comes," he advises young people today. Colin Powell's own life proves the truth of that advice.

Chapter 2

Moving Up

Opportunity knocked on very few doors in the 1930s. It was a time of economic hardship known as the Great Depression, and many Americans were barely managing to make ends meet. No one struggled more than the residents of Harlem, the neighborhood in northern New York City where Colin Powell was born. As African Americans, the people of Harlem had to confront the added problem of racial prejudice.

Finding good jobs had always been hard for black Americans. The Great Depression made it even harder. Twenty-five percent of the nation's work force was unemployed. In Harlem, 80 percent of the workers could not find jobs. People worried about paying the rent, buying clothes, and having enough food to eat.

Many Harlem residents had fled racial hatred in the South, hoping to find better treatment in the North. If life was better in New York City, however, it was not much better.

People in white neighborhoods would not rent or sell homes to African Americans. Blacks were not served in many of the stores and restaurants that white people used. They were not even allowed to enter the Harlem nightclubs that white New Yorkers liked to visit.

Luther and Maud Powell, Colin's parents, felt lucky to have jobs during these hard times. Luther worked as a shipping clerk while his wife earned money as a seamstress. The Powells had come to the United States from the West Indian nation of Jamaica, determined to build a better life. When their son, Colin Luther, was born on April 5, 1937, they vowed that he would receive a good education. He would get a steady job and escape the worries that so many people faced.

In 1940, the Powells moved to another New York City neighborhood, the Hunts Point area of the South Bronx. With their parents at work all day, Colin and his older sister, Marilyn, were among the first "latch-key kids," Colin Powell recalled. Although the children came home from school to

This Harlem street scene is typical of the neighborhood where Colin Powell spent the earliest years of his life.

an empty apartment, they rarely felt lonely. The Powell children grew up near many relatives and friends—what Powell called a "floating family."

"I lived in a big extended family," Colin Powell said, "where everybody got together, especially on Thanksgiving and Christmas. These two holidays were a very important time for us. Aunts, uncles, and cousins would all be there. We would assemble either around the table or in front of the couch and have our picture taken."

Today, those holiday photographs are among the family's treasured possessions. "It brings back many fond memories to see those pictures over a 30-year time frame and see the changes from year to year," Powell remarked.

In Hunts Point, there was always a cousin or playmate to help Colin pass the time. Colin and his best friend, Gene Norman, bought square hamburgers at the White Castle restaurant. They played stickball, a city street game, and raced their bicycles up and down Kelly Street, where the Powells lived.

"The favorite pastime of the kids on my block was what we called 'making the walk,'" Powell said. "We would start at the corner of Kelly Street, walk up 163rd Street, around Southern Boulevard to Westchester, then back down Westchester to

Kelly Street." As an adult, Powell remembered that the walk "was an exciting thing to do because there were toy stores at every corner on Westchester, Southern Boulevard had three big movies, and all along the way were small and large stores selling almost every product one could want."

In summer, the children flew kites from the roofs of their apartment buildings. On the hot city sidewalks, they tossed marbles against cigar boxes and filled bottle caps with wax to make checkers.

Life in Hunts Point introduced Colin to a rich variety of people and cultures. "Ours was a neighborhood of young blacks and Puerto Ricans, mixed with a large Jewish population," he observed.

In the corner grocery stores, clerks greeted their customers in Spanish. In other shops, merchants chatted in Yiddish, a language spoken by many Jewish immigrants. Colin learned early in life to feel at ease with people from different backgrounds. He even spoke some Yiddish—just "*ein bissel*" (a little), he said.

This mixture of people and their traditions also helped to protect Colin and Marilyn Powell from much of the pain of racism. "I didn't know I was a minority," Colin remarked, "because everybody was a minority."

Colin Powell (second from right) and his friends liked to roam the city streets near their homes, enjoying the mixture of people and traditions in Hunts Point.

But Hunts Point did not shield the youngsters from all the hazards of growing up. Colin and his friend Gene were smart enough to stay clear of one street corner, a spot where drugs were sold. "We knew about marijuana and heroin. We knew it was used around the neighborhood," Colin said as an adult. "But for those of us secure in our family lives, that wasn't tolerated."

Colin was also aware of troublesome events outside of Hunts Point. His earliest memories are of World War II. He was four years old when the war started. As a boy, Colin saw many young men from Hunts Point—black, white, and Hispanic—going off to fight. He still remembers the news reports that he heard about a hero who shared his first name, Captain Colin Kelly. A World War II pilot, Kelly died when his plane was shot down following an attack on a Japanese battleship.

Colin Powell was a teen-ager when America went to war again, this time as part of a force sent to Korea. "I grew up in a time of wars," he said.

It pleased Maud and Luther Powell to see Colin growing up healthy and happy—and staying out of trouble. The Powells expected their son to be an achiever. "Make something of your life," his parents said. "Strive for a good education."

Colin's father and mother both believed that education was the door to opportunity. "Books and newspapers were very much a part of my home," Powell recalled.

Years earlier, Luther Powell had been forced to quit school to earn a living. Without much formal education, his job options, or choices, were limited. He wanted his children to graduate from high school and go on to college. He wanted them to have more options in life.

Maud Powell took great pride in the fact that she had finished high school. "In any family discussion, when my mother occasionally got annoyed at my father," Colin Powell said, "she would remind everyone that she was the high-school graduate."

Although Colin's parents urged him to study, he did not care about his lessons. He did so poorly, in fact, that in the fifth grade Colin was placed in a class for slow learners. Colin's attitude did not change when he entered Morris High School. He "horsed around a lot," he said, and preferred sports to studying. Running through Van Cortlandt Park with his friends on the track team was more fun than doing homework.

In 1954, when he was 18, Colin entered the City College of New York. He settled on geology,

Colin Powell poses with his parents and sister at her graduation from college in 1952.

A Pershing Rifles drill team practices in 1958. When Colin Powell saw the Pershing Rifles at City College, he was inspired to join them.

or earth science, as the main subject that he would study. But geology did not interest him any more than his other classes. He had not discovered a subject that captured his interest or made him want to excel.

Colin Powell can recall the day when he first saw the Pershing Rifles, a precision marching team. As cadets in the Reserve Officers Training Corps (ROTC), these City College students were learning to be Army officers. The cadets wore white gloves with their black uniforms, and their brass buttons gleamed in the sunlight. They moved in unison as a commander crisply called out orders: "Company, attention!" "Present arms!" "Left shoulder arms!" "Forward march!"

Powell watched the drill team with excitement. "That was my option," he realized. Colin decided to join the ROTC program. Like Colin Kelly and the servicemen from Hunts Point, Colin Powell would be a soldier.

With this goal before him, Colin began to work hard. In his ROTC classes, he studied military history and combat tactics. He trained outdoors on tough obstacle courses. And Colin experienced a new feeling, a feeling of confidence and pride in his accomplishments.

Colin encouraged other students to excel, too. Appointed commander of the Pershing Rifles, he learned the skills that make a good leader. Colin set high standards for his squad—and high standards for himself. "When you find something you're good at, you tend to pursue it," Colin Powell said.

"I don't know if I would have finished City College," Colin Powell admitted, "had it not been for ROTC." But he did finish college. In fact, he graduated in 1958 with the highest grades in his ROTC class. Powell also reached the highest rank in the Corps—cadet colonel—and was named a "distinguished military graduate." The Army gave Colin Powell his first taste of success—and he made the most of that opportunity.

Colin Powell became a member of the Pershing Rifles and, later, their commander.

Chapter 3

Loyalty

After graduation, Colin Powell headed for Fort Benning, Georgia, home of the country's largest military post. Now a second lieutenant, Powell was ready to begin three years of active duty in the U.S. Army.

Powell would go on to have a distinguished military career. But he is only one of many African Americans who have served in the U.S. military.

Seven thousand African Americans served in the U.S. Army and Navy during the American Revolution. The first person killed in that war was a runaway slave named Crispus Attucks. He died in Boston in 1770, when British soldiers shot into a crowd of angry colonists.

People of African descent fought in every important battle in the Revolution. A former slave named Peter Salem earned a place in American history during the Battle of Bunker Hill. As the

British major John Pitcairn led his troops against the Americans, Salem saw his chance to shoot. "The day is ours!" Pitcairn cried. Moments later, Salem shot him dead. A plaque at Bunker Hill honors Peter Salem as a "soldier of the Revolution."

Thousands of African-American men served on land and sea during the War of 1812, when Americans again fought British soldiers. From Lake Erie to New Orleans, black soldiers won praise for their courage and loyalty. "Soldiers, you surpass my hopes," said General Andrew Jackson to the black men under his command.

The African-American sailors on Commander Nathaniel Shaler's ship fought bravely even after being wounded. Shaler singled out a "black man by the name of John Johnson," who shouted encouragement to his fellow seamen as he lay dying on the deck. Johnson deserved a place in "the book of fame," according to Commander Shaler. "While America has such tars [sailors]," Shaler remarked, "she has little to fear from the tyrants of the ocean."

In peacetime, though, the armed forces failed to welcome African Americans. After the Revolutionary War, the U.S. Congress limited military service to "able-bodied white males." Soon after the War of 1812, the Army issued an order stating,

"No Negro . . . will be received as a recruit." White Americans were quick to forget the sacrifices of black fighting men.

When civil war broke out in 1861, African Americans were once again denied the opportunity to serve their country. Not until 1863 did Congress permit the Army to enlist black soldiers. The high death toll had created a desperate need for more soldiers, and black men were asked to fight for their country. They answered that call to arms.

Northern states formed black regiments, fighting units of black men under the command of white officers. More than 186,000 black men served in 166 such units. They were known as the United States Colored Troops.

Volunteers from several states and Canada formed the best known of these regiments, the 54th Massachusetts Colored Infantry. On July 18, 1863, the 54th Infantry was chosen to lead the attack on Fort Wagner in South Carolina. The men of the 54th knew that they were not just fighting another Civil War battle. They had to prove that black men could fight for their country.

The attack won praise for the courage of the regiment and made a hero of Sergeant William Carney. Carney bravely carried his country's flag

to the very front of the attack. Even after being wounded, he made sure that the flag never touched the ground. For his heroism under fire, William Carney became the first African American to earn the Congressional Medal of Honor. Sixteen other black soldiers and sailors received the Medal of Honor for their service during the Civil War. And more than 37,000 black Americans lost their lives in the conflict.

This woodcut depicts an African-American regiment marching into Charleston, South Carolina, during the Civil War.

After the Civil War, African-American soldiers were made part of the peacetime Army for the first time. The 9th and 10th cavalries, two groups of black soldiers on horseback, were formed at Fort Leavenworth, Kansas. These men, known as Buffalo Soldiers, served on the Western frontier and in the Spanish-American War (1898).

But the place given to black soldiers by the Army remained a second-class one. There were few African-American officers, for instance. Although blacks had demonstrated their ability to fight, most military leaders did not believe that they were able to command combat troops.

The Army also continued to keep blacks in segregated units, where they were often assigned only the most routine tasks.

More than 400,000 blacks joined the Army during the First World War. Though few of these soldiers ever saw combat, those who did performed with valor.

One of these men was Private Henry Johnson of Albany, New York, who belonged to the 369th Regiment, a black division sent to fight in France. Johnson received three wounds when the German army attacked his division, yet he kept on fighting until the Germans retreated. He also rescued one of his fellow soldiers, Private Needham Roberts, who had been captured while resisting the attack. Johnson and Roberts became the first Americans, black or white, to receive the *Croix de Guerre*, a French medal of honor.

By the time the United States entered World War II in December 1941, the nation had its first black general, Benjamin O. Davis, Sr. American fighting forces in World War II included a million African-American men and women. Among these black soldiers was General Davis's son, Benjamin O. Davis, Jr., who commanded the first African-American pilots, the "Black Eagles" of the 99th Pursuit Squadron. The skill and patriotism shown by these servicemen helped to persuade President Harry S Truman to integrate the military in 1948.

Ten years later, Colin Powell joined a military force in which blacks and whites worked side by side. He joined a force in which black officers were allowed to command troops. At Fort Benning, as in Hunts Point, Powell found that people did not judge him by his race.

"In the Army, I never felt I was looked down on by my white colleagues," he said. "I've been given the opportunity to compete fair and square with them."

Benjamin O. Davis, Sr., and his son speak at a news conference during World War II.

At Fort Benning, Powell joined the Ranger Training Brigade. Powell learned to survive as an infantryman, or foot soldier, in enemy territory. The Rangers parachuted from planes and hiked far into the wilderness. They built rope bridges across streams and climbed up and down mountains. As a Ranger, Powell received instruction in infantry

A Ranger undergoes rugged training on the ropes course.

combat techniques, such as setting ambushes and handling explosives. His broad shoulders often carried a heavy machine gun for the group.

Ranger training taught Colin Powell more than wilderness survival and combat skills. A successful Ranger developed the personal qualities that Powell read about in the *Ranger Handbook*: "loyalty to the nation's ideals, loyalty to unit, selfless service, and personal responsibility." Powell was remembered by his fellow Rangers for those qualities. As in ROTC, he proved himself to be a strong leader, able to take charge and help others succeed.

Powell's sense of loyalty was returned by the men of his unit. When they had a free evening, Powell and his fellow Rangers liked to go out and enjoy themselves. Often, they went to taverns in the towns around Fort Benning. At first, the bartenders wouldn't serve an African American.

One of the men in Powell's unit, William Mc-Caffrey, recalled how the Rangers refused to accept this kind of treatment. "This is our Ranger partner. You have to serve him!" they insisted. "And they would," McCaffrey remembered.

Throughout the South, people were challenging segregation in other ways. At that time, the South had laws requiring separate public facilities

Under the South's Jim Crow laws, landlords prevented African Americans from renting apartments by posting signs like this one.

for blacks and whites. Known as Jim Crow laws, these rules created separate worlds—one for whites, one for blacks. Blacks could not eat at restaurants open to whites. They could not sit next to whites in movie theaters. They could not even drink from the water fountains marked "Whites Only."

Years earlier, the U.S. Supreme Court ruled that this kind of segregation was legal as long as public services were "separate but equal." Across the South, however, the public facilities enjoyed by white communities were far better than those provided to blacks. The southern worlds of black and white were separate and unequal.

In the late 1950s, as Colin Powell practiced combat skills, African Americans across the South were demanding equal treatment and opportunity. Often joined by white civil rights workers, blacks protested the racist practices that trapped them in second-class citizenship.

In 1954, the Supreme Court reversed its earlier decision. In a case known as *Brown v. Board of Education*, the Court ruled that segregated public school systems violated the Constitution. "In the field of public education, the doctrine of 'separate but equal' has no place," pronounced Chief Justice Earl Warren.

For years after that, however, most southern school districts ignored the court's decision. The governor of Arkansas promised that "blood will run in the streets" if black students tried to attend all-white Central High School in the city of Little Rock. In 1957, President Dwight D. Eisenhower was forced to send federal troops to Little Rock to protect nine black teen-agers who wanted to attend Central High.

African Americans demanded equal treatment in public transportation, too. In December 1955, a seamstress named Rosa Parks refused to give up her seat on a Montgomery, Alabama, bus to let a white man sit down. After the police arrested Parks, a young minister, Martin Luther King, Jr., led a boycott of the city's buses. "We will not retreat one inch in our fight to secure and hold onto our American citizenship," King announced.

For 13 months, the city's African Americans refused to use the city's buses. They would ride the buses again, they said, when people were seated without regard to race. The boycotters won their fight when the Supreme Court outlawed segregated buses in December 1956.

At Fort Benning, Powell followed the news about the growing civil rights movement. But the

Army soon sent the young second lieutenant far away from events at home. In 1958, Powell was assigned as a platoon leader at an American Army post in West Germany. By 1960, he was back in the United States at Fort Devens, Massachusetts.

One evening, some of Colin Powell's friends arranged a date for him with a young woman from Birmingham, Alabama. Alma Johnson had come to Boston to study speech therapy. The two liked each other right away. "He was absolutely the nicest person I ever met," Alma later said.

She was surprised, though, when she learned that Colin intended to make the Army his career. "Everyone else I knew in the Army had the days and minutes of their remaining service counted," Alma recalled.

After he became chairman of the Joint Chiefs of Staff, people often asked Colin Powell when he had decided to stay in the Army. "I don't recall ever reaching a momentous point where I had to consciously decide whether or not I was going to continue to serve in the military," he replied. "I have always enjoyed being in the Army, and as the years went by, I continued to be challenged with each new assignment. I simply had no desire to do anything else."

Chapter 4

In His Own Way

When Maud and Luther Powell saw their son in early 1962, they learned that he had been given a new assignment. The Army was sending him to the small Asian nation of South Vietnam. "They had never heard of the place," Colin Powell said. "We looked it up on a map."

Colin married Alma on August 25, 1962, a few months before he was due to be shipped out. Although it meant leaving his new wife, Powell looked forward to this assignment. "This was hot stuff," he said. "It was action."

The action was about 7,600 miles from the U.S. mainland. For many years, Vietnam had been a single colony governed by France. In 1954, the Vietnamese had won their independence, but they could not agree on how to govern their country.

A communist force took control of the north while an anti-communist government arose in the south. The two sides were soon at war, and South Vietnam called on the United States for help. President John F. Kennedy agreed to send a force of 16,000 military advisers, including Powell, to Vietnam.

While Powell was in Vietnam, Alma, who was pregnant, stayed with her family in Birmingham. "For me, at that time, going home was the best alternative," she said. "That's where my support system was."

A sign in Birmingham welcomed visitors to "The Magic City." For Birmingham's black residents, however, there was nothing magical about the city.

Martin Luther King, Jr., called Birmingham "the most thoroughly segregated city in the United States." After the U.S. government ordered an end to segregated public facilities, Birmingham's white leaders closed the city's parks, swimming pools, and playgrounds rather than open them to blacks.

By the time Alma Powell arrived there in 1962, Birmingham had become the site of numerous civil rights demonstrations. Protesters often met with violence. City police used clubs and cattle prods to frighten unarmed marchers. Demonstrators were

blasted with streams of water from fire hoses—water sprayed so forcefully that it tore the bark from trees. Television reports showed the horrifying image of police dogs attacking defenseless people. Far away in Vietnam, Colin Powell worried about Alma.

But Powell also followed the news of the civil rights movement with great interest. On August 28, 1963, Martin Luther King, Jr., and other civil rights leaders marched at the head of a crowd of 250,000 people. They had come to Washington, D.C., from every part of the country to demand

Civil rights protesters continued to march for equal rights despite attempts by the police to break up demonstrations.

equal treatment for African Americans. "I have a dream today!" King told the crowd. "I have a dream that my four little children will one day live in a nation where they will not be judged by the color of their skin, but by the content of their character."

To Powell, King's words promised freedom for all Americans. "Abraham Lincoln freed the slaves, but it was Martin Luther King who freed the whites, who freed the American people," Powell insisted. "The real Civil War was fought in the 1960s—as important as the battles fought in the 1860s—to free Americans from segregation a hundred years after freeing the slaves."

Martin Luther King, Jr., addresses a crowd of hundreds of thousands in Washington, D.C., in 1963.

Powell wished that he could take part in the civil rights struggle at home. "Because of my position and the things I was doing in my life, I didn't have a chance to participate in that struggle in an active way," he explained.

However, he found another way to participate, by setting an example for others. "I did it in my own way, by my own example and by helping other people who were coming along as best I could," Powell remarked. His own success, Powell believed, showed other black soldiers that it was possible to succeed through hard work and a positive outlook. "If you have a loser's attitude going in, you will come out a loser," he insisted.

News from home reached Colin Powell slowly. In 1963, as he patrolled the jungles of South Vietnam, Powell was often far from radios, newspapers, and telephones. He did not learn he was a father until his son, Michael, was two weeks old.

A few weeks later, as Powell led a group of South Vietnamese soldiers through a rice field, he stepped on a punji-stick trap. Set by the North Vietnamese, the trap sent a sharpened bamboo stick through Powell's foot. It took weeks for the painful injury to heal, but Powell was soon back on patrol. For his work in Vietnam, he received the Purple

"The real Civil War was fought in the 1960s—as important as the battles fought in the 1860s—to free Americans from segregation a hundred years after freeing the slaves."

35

In 1963, Colin Powell received the Purple Heart, a medal awarded to servicemen wounded in action.

Heart, a medal awarded to soldiers injured in battle, and the Bronze Star, for valor.

After he finished his assignment in Vietnam, Powell returned to Fort Benning and family life. Alma was a volunteer in Fort Benning's military hospital, working for the Red Cross. When Michael was two years old, a second child, Linda, was born.

Colin Powell also returned to racial prejudice. Only weeks after Martin Luther King, Jr., spoke of his dream of equality to the American people, a bomb exploded in a Birmingham church, killing four black children. Alma's father bought a shotgun to protect his family.

At times, Powell personally faced the humiliation of racist attitudes. One afternoon, he stopped at a restaurant in Columbus, Georgia, and ordered a hamburger. The waitress told Powell that she would not serve him inside the restaurant. You will have to get your food at the back door, she said.

The Powells escaped that kind of treatment when they traveled to Fort Leavenworth, Kansas. Known as the home of the Buffalo Soldiers, Fort Leavenworth was the headquarters of the Army Command and Staff College. The college offered advanced training for Army commanders. There, Powell learned how to plan military campaigns.

He also began to think about getting a graduate degree in business administration. A degree in business could open up new opportunities in the Army, he thought. But Powell was told by his commanding officer that his college grades weren't good enough.

Colin Powell couldn't accept that. Believing that "hard work generates good luck—and opportunities," Powell labored over his studies at the staff college. High grades, he hoped, would persuade the Army to send him to business school.

As usual, Colin Powell pushed himself to do his best—and as usual, he met the tough standards that he set for himself. Of the 1,244 officers who graduated from Fort Leavenworth with Powell, only one received better grades.

But Powell had to wait for the opportunity to continue his education. The Army had decided to send him back to Vietnam. In the years since he had returned from Vietnam, the war had grown into an international conflict. The United States was aiding the South Vietnamese while China and the Soviet Union supported the north.

By 1968, when Colin Powell returned to Vietnam, nearly half a million American soldiers were stationed there. More than 50,000 of them were African Americans.

African Americans in Vietnam observe the birthday of Martin Luther King, Jr.

General William Westmoreland, commander of American forces in South Vietnam, proclaimed that the black soldier had "come into his own." He meant that for the first time, black soldiers enjoyed equal opportunity and responsibility.

However, many people argued that black soldiers shouldered more than their share of the hard work and danger in Vietnam. Though blacks made up only 11 percent of the U.S. population, they accounted for 23 percent of the deaths in Vietnam. They were more likely to face dangerous combat assignments. There were few black officers.

But as in America's previous wars, the black soldier responded to military duty with courage and honor. Twenty Congressional Medals of Honor for heroism during the Vietnam War went to African-American soldiers.

Colin Powell served two tours of duty in Vietnam during the 1960s.

In Vietnam, Colin Powell's hard work at last generated some good luck—and an opportunity. The *Army Times* printed an article about the five top students in the recent staff college class. When the company commander saw Powell's picture on the page, he simply couldn't believe his eyes. "I've got the number two Leavenworth graduate in my division—and he's stuck in the boonies?" the commander shouted. "I want him on my staff!"

That decision was a stepping stone in Powell's military career. It also saved the commander's life. Powell was with the commander on a helicopter mission in the jungle-covered mountains of Vietnam when the pilot tried to land in a small clearing. Suddenly, one of the helicopter's rotor blades hit a tree and stopped turning. "Once that happens, the helicopter is a rock," Powell said.

As the chopper fell to the earth, Powell readied himself for the crash. "I bent over and put my hands under my knees," he recalled.

As soon as the copter hit the ground, Powell got out and ran. He wanted to be far from the helicopter if its gas tank exploded. Then he remembered the others inside the craft. "I turned around and realized the helicopter was starting to smoke while the men were still in there," he said.

Helicopters were used frequently by the Americans in the jungles of Vietnam.

40

Risking his own life, Powell returned to the helicopter and pulled out his commander, who was nearly unconscious. Powell continued to rescue the soldiers. "I went in and got the chief of staff out," he remembered. "He had a concussion. Then I went back to get an aide, who we thought was dead." The aide turned out to be alive, but injured. "As I unbuckled him, he moaned," Powell said. "We got him out and pulled off his helmet. It was all bent out of shape, but it saved his life." The pilot of the helicopter was also rescued.

Colin Powell's bravery that day earned him the Soldier's Medal, an award for heroic action. But Powell brought away from that episode something more valuable.

On a mountain in Vietnam, he discovered—firsthand—the source of true heroism. As Colin Powell himself said, "It comes from caring about the people you're with."

Chapter 5

A Complete Soldier

Powell returned from Vietnam in July of 1969. He enrolled at George Washington University in Washington, D.C., to study business administration. When he wasn't studying, he could be found in the garage tinkering with old cars. He and Alma liked to relax in front of the television. "Alma and I particularly enjoy watching old movies together," Powell said.

He also found time to play with Michael and Linda, and before long, he was changing the diapers of a new baby, Annemarie. As busy as he was, Colin Powell always made time for his family.

"Although my career has required hard work and long hours through the years, Alma and I have always made a concerted effort to spend quality time with Michael, Linda, and Annemarie," Powell recently explained. "That's the way we grew up, and we wanted the same for our children. I have many fond memories of vacations together, and weekends are still a special time for the family to get together."

"We never felt that his work was more important than we were," Linda remembers.

Like many military families, the Powells moved often. During the 1970s and 1980s, his Army career took Colin Powell from one assignment to another. With each new assignment, he took on more and more responsibility.

In 1972, Colin Powell was one of 17 people selected from more than 1,500 candidates to serve as White House Fellows. These special assistants get experience in government offices. Powell went to work at the Office of Management and Budget, where he helped to prepare the nation's budget. He also worked for the departments of energy and defense during the succeeding years. From 1981 to 1985, Powell served as a military assistant to the Secretary of Defense, Caspar Weinberger.

Between such government assignments, Powell commanded soldiers both overseas and at home. In every job, Powell's hard work and dedication impressed his bosses. He put in long, tiring days.

Powell was "a superb soldier," according to Caspar Weinberger, "a great patriot in the best and truest sense of the word." Weinberger wasn't the only one who thought so. During these years, Powell received a series of promotions in rank—from major to colonel, brigadier general, major general, and lieutenant general.

Whether he was reviewing military strategies or looking over a department budget, Colin Powell never forgot how it felt to be a soldier in the field. He enjoyed casual chats with men and women of all ranks and backgrounds.

"If there ever was anybody who could communicate with a private fixing a broken tire tread and in the next second talk with the president," said one of his colleagues, "it's Colin Powell."

Powell expected all young soldiers to strive for excellence, just as he had. In 1973, the Army sent Powell to Korea to take charge of the First Battalion, 32nd Infantry, a unit that had experienced serious problems. Black and white soldiers in the battalion were fighting with each other. Many were using drugs.

Powell demanded that these soldiers do their best—and that did not include fights or drugs. He went to work at once to make changes. "I threw

the bums out of the Army and put the drug users in jail," he said. "The rest we ran four miles every morning, and by night they were too tired to get into trouble."

But Powell was more than a stern commander who could whip troublesome troops into shape. His actions also showed that he cared deeply about the soldiers he commanded.

In 1976, Colin Powell took on a new command at Fort Campbell, Kentucky. One of his battalion leaders, Lieutenant Colonel Vic Michael, slipped

Powell rides a jeep in Korea, where he was stationed from 1973 to 1974.

and hurt his back while getting out of a helicopter. Michael needed a long period of recovery.

Another commander might have replaced the injured battalion leader. But Powell held Michael's job open for him until he returned. "Powell could have ended my career, but he had faith in me," Michael said. "I never will forget his understanding for me as a soldier and a human being."

Colin Powell also had a deep appreciation for the soldiers who came before him, particularly those who were African American. In 1982, Powell was back at Fort Leavenworth, serving as deputy commander. While jogging one morning, he noticed that some gravel alleys on the base were named 9th and 10th Cavalry streets, after the Buffalo Soldiers. "I wonder if that's all there is," Powell said to himself. He found it hard to believe that two alleys were the only memorial to those dedicated African-American soldiers.

When Colin Powell learned that there was no other monument to the Buffalo Soldiers, he started a project to create one. "That was a situation that had to be changed," he said. The new monument would be built at Fort Leavenworth, "in the center of the region where both the 9th and 10th cavalries spent so much of their blood."

Carlton Philpot, a Navy commander who was interested in the Buffalo Soldiers, took over the monument project when Powell moved on to his next assignment. A sculptor named Eddie Dixon designed a 16-foot statue of a soldier on horseback for the monument site. It would stand near a marker listing the 20 Buffalo Soldiers who received the Congressional Medal of Honor.

By 1986, Powell called himself "probably the happiest general in the world." Not only could he look back on 28 years of service in the Army, he also looked forward to new career challenges.

His family made him proud as well. The three Powell children, now young adults, were headed toward success in their chosen fields. Michael, a first lieutenant in the Army, was stationed in Germany. Linda hoped to be an actress. The youngest child, Annemarie, was looking forward to college.

Soon, however, a crisis struck the Powell family. In 1987, Michael was in an automobile accident in Germany. Colin and Alma were alarmed to learn that Michael was seriously injured. If Michael survived, his doctors said, he would spend his life in a wheelchair.

The Army flew Michael to Walter Reed Army Medical Center, in Washington, D.C., for surgery.

Before the operation and throughout a long hospital stay, Colin Powell gave his son strong words of encouragement. "You'll make it," he said. "You want to make it, so you *will* make it!"

With his father urging him on, Michael Powell learned to walk with a cane. A few years after his accident, Michael had built a new life. Relieved of his Army duties, he prepared for a law career. Michael married his girlfriend from college, and the couple had a baby boy. Colin Powell, the proud new grandfather, found his grandson to be "quite a charming little devil."

In 1987, Colin Powell was appointed as the nation's national security adviser. In this job, he gave President Ronald Reagan advice about foreign policy matters and kept him informed about the readiness of America's forces. "As national security adviser, I had the opportunity to brief President Reagan each morning on important issues facing America," Powell explained.

Colin Powell was proud to be the first African-American national security adviser. He was equally proud of the tradition of African-American service to country. Facing a new career challenge, Powell looked back at the black men and women who had come before him, people who had worked and

Powell became President Reagan's national security adviser in 1987.

sacrificed to improve his opportunities. They were "men and women of enormous potential," he said, "who, because of prejudice and intolerance, were not allowed to make their full contribution to this great country."

As national security adviser, Powell consulted with the secretaries of state and defense on foreign policy issues. He reported to members of Congress about events that concerned the security of the nation. Working to reduce tensions between the United States and the Soviet Union, Powell helped to plan summit meetings between President Reagan and Soviet President Mikhail Gorbachev.

For his work as national security adviser, Colin Powell received the Distinguished Service Award.

Powell served as national security adviser until 1989, when Reagan's second term ended. George Bush, the new president, wanted to choose his own person for the job. Shortly before Bush took the Oath of Office, Colin Powell gave his final report to President Reagan.

"Mr. President," Powell said, "the world is at peace." It was the kind of report that a soldier is most happy to give.

Near the end of his term as national security adviser, Colin and Alma Powell attended a formal dinner at the White House. An African-American waiter approached Powell during the meal. "I just wanted to thank you and say it's been good to see you here," the waiter told Powell. "I was in World War II, and I fought all the way from North Africa to Italy."

"Brother," Colin Powell replied, "I ought to be thanking you!"

Chapter 6

The Price
of Readiness

Colin Powell had reached a crossroads in his life. Out of a job, he had to decide what to do with his future. Should he stay in the Army, he wondered, or should he retire?

As Powell weighed his decision, he made two columns on a sheet of paper. Powell labeled them "Reasons to Stay in the Army" and "Reasons to Leave the Army." He quickly listed many reasons to stay. Army life still challenged him to succeed. It gave him a chance to serve his country, to lead young soldiers, and to be a role model for African-American youth. After 30 years, the Army was his home.

When it came time to list his reasons for leaving, though, Powell came up with only one. He could make much more money by giving lectures about his military career. For Powell, that was not good enough. He decided to stay in the Army.

In early 1989, Powell was promoted to the rank of general. Wearing four silver stars on his uniform, he held the highest military rank in the United States at that time. He took over Forces Command at Fort McPherson, Georgia, the Army's biggest combat unit. More than one million soldiers were under his command.

But only a few months later, while on a trip to Washington, D.C., the general called his wife in Georgia with the news that he had a new job. "Alma," he said, "we are moving again." The president had appointed Colin Powell to the highest military position in the country, chairman of the Joint Chiefs of Staff.

"General Powell has had a truly distinguished military career, and he's a complete soldier," Bush stated. "He will bring leadership, insight, and wisdom to our efforts to keep the military strong."

"Mr. President, I'm ready to go to it," Powell replied. "I look forward to the challenges ahead."

At 52, Powell was the youngest person ever to hold this position. As the first African-American chairman, he became a hero to young blacks both in and out of the military. "It's been a great source

Colin Powell is sworn in as chairman of the Joint Chiefs of Staff by Secretary of Defense Dick Cheney, as Alma Powell holds the Bible.

of pride to walk into a store and have a black young man come up and say, 'I just wanted to shake your hand,' " the chairman said.

Colin Powell's first day as chairman of the Joint Chiefs was October 3, 1989. That afternoon, the Pentagon employees—20,000 men and women—poured out of the building's doors. They stood outside in a strong fall wind, filling the Pentagon's courtyard, to welcome their new boss.

As Powell looked upon the crowd, he spoke of a painting that hung in a Pentagon hallway. The painting showed a family in church, kneeling to pray. The father in the painting wore a uniform.

"You can sense from the painting that the family is praying together one last time before the father goes off to war," Powell said. "Every time I pass that painting, a silent prayer comes to mind for all those who serve this nation in times of danger."

As the new chairman of the Joint Chiefs of Staff, Powell wanted what every soldier wants— peace. On that windy October day, he hoped that "the men and women of our armed forces will pay only the price of eternal readiness, and not the tragic and precious price of life."

But Powell had been chairman for only a short time when he had to ask American soldiers to pay that tragic price.

The United States was deeply concerned about General Manuel Noriega, a man Powell called a "tough hombre." The leader of Panama, a Central American nation, Noriega had ignored the results of free elections and ruled the country as a dictator. He was also suspected of letting drug dealers use Panama as a shipping point to the United States.

Then, in December of 1989, Noriega's soldiers shot and killed a U.S. Marine. They also beat and tortured an American Navy lieutenant. The U.S. government feared that the Americans living in Panama—13,000 soldiers and their families—were in danger. President Bush asked Powell to develop plans for a surprise attack on Panama.

To Colin Powell, the decision to use armed force against Noriega had to be made carefully. "We should not go around saying that we are the world's policeman," he cautioned. But it was clear to him that, in this case, force had to be used.

Powell and his staff began to plan an assault on Panama's defense forces. "You're going to have American blood spilled," he warned the president. Such an attack would mean American deaths and injuries. But Powell assured the president, "We will do everything we can to keep them at a minimum."

Hours before the sun rose on December 20, 1989, Powell gave the signal to launch Operation Just Cause. Twenty-four thousand soldiers stormed Panama in a surprise nighttime invasion. American forces quickly destroyed Noriega's headquarters and key military posts. On January 3, 1990, Noriega himself surrendered to the United States.

Powell congratulates an officer who joined in the assault on the defense forces headquarters in Panama.

With his first crisis as chairman of the Joint Chiefs behind him, Powell had time for a more pleasant duty. On July 28, 1990, he stood before a crowd of people on a Kansas hillside. Colin Powell had returned to Fort Leavenworth to celebrate the groundbreaking of the Buffalo Soldier Monument.

Harry Hollowell and Elisha Kearse, both former Buffalo Soldiers, sat near Powell as he spoke. On this occasion, Powell's thoughts again turned to pictures of America's military heritage. He told the crowd about three paintings that hung in his Pentagon office. They depicted the illustrious deeds of the Buffalo Soldiers: patrolling the West on horseback, scouting the Great Plains, fighting in the Spanish-American War.

The paintings, said Powell, "remind me of my heritage and of the thousands of African Americans who went before me and made sacrifices so that I could sit in that office today."

Days later, Colin Powell was back in his office at the Pentagon. Another crisis was at hand. As Powell sat beneath the paintings of past military heroes, thousands of American men and women were beginning the journey to Saudi Arabia.

Chapter 7

A Desert Storm

On military bases across the United States, the men and women of America's armed forces dressed themselves in their desert fatigues—mottled brown clothing that would make them less visible in the Saudi Arabian desert. They said good-bye to loved ones and boarded ships and planes headed for the Middle East.

These soldiers were preparing to face the army of Saddam Hussein, an army that was now digging in at the Saudi Arabian border.

The American government acted quickly to protect Saudi Arabia. "The sooner we put something in place to deter, the better off we are," Colin Powell had told the president. "We cannot allow that kind of aggression to exist in the world these days." The United States positioned tanks and jet

In 1990, huge transport planes carried thousands of American troops to Saudi Arabia.

fighters in the Saudi Arabian desert. Battleships were sent to the Persian Gulf. Operation Desert Shield—the campaign to protect Saudi Arabia— had begun.

Three months after Iraqi troops raced across the border with Kuwait, 180,000 Americans had

been deployed to the Persian Gulf. Huge transport planes brought in billions of pounds of equipment and supplies. They carried everything from bottles of sunscreen, needed to shield the soldiers from the strong desert sunlight, to protective suits, in case the Iraqis attacked with chemical weapons.

The Iraqi leader, Saddam Hussein, predicted that American troops would face "the mother of all battles."

Nations throughout the world had condemned Iraq's actions. The United Nations (U.N.) called for an economic embargo—an agreement that U.N. members would not sell goods to Iraq. The United States and other nations blockaded Iraq's coastline with naval vessels so ships could not get in or out.

With troops, weapons, and economic sanctions in place, the world watched to see what Saddam Hussein would do. At the Pentagon, Colin Powell hoped that the military build-up would prevent an attack on Saudi Arabia. The economic sanctions, he hoped, would eventually force Iraq to retreat.

But the Iraqi soldiers did not pull back. Instead, Saddam Hussein strengthened his communication and supply lines. By October, Hussein had 430,000 soldiers in Kuwait, and his army set about destroying the country.

Iraqi soldiers tortured and killed many Kuwaiti citizens. They ransacked government buildings and set fire to stores and hotels. They took anything of value, from toys to television sets, from air conditioners to computers. They stole every book from the library of Kuwait University.

The reports of this destruction convinced President Bush that stopping the Iraqis at the Saudi Arabian border would not be enough. They must be driven out of Kuwait before nothing was left of the country. "This will not stand, this aggression against Kuwait," Bush promised the world.

Powell wanted President Bush to wait for non-offensive methods to work. The sanctions and naval blockade, he believed, would slowly strangle Iraq. In time, this policy of containment would force its army out of Kuwait.

Over his long career, Powell had gathered a set of "Rules to Live By"—sayings that often guided his actions. One of those rules reminded him, "Be careful what you choose. You might get it."

Colin Powell hoped that President Bush would think very carefully before choosing the course that could lead to war.

Powell decided to raise these concerns to the president. On a sunny October day, he met with Bush and his top advisers in the White House. Powell sat up straight on the edge of his chair. As he spoke, the president listened closely.

"There is a case here for the containment, or strangulation, policy," Powell stated. He said that the forces in Saudi Arabia already had the Iraqi army boxed in. "This is an option that has merit," Powell told the president. "It may take a year, it may take two years. But it will work some day."

President Bush warned the Iraqis, "This will not stand, this aggression against Kuwait."

President Bush, however, was not certain that peaceful methods would drive Saddam Hussein's army back. He worried that other nations would break the blockade and start selling goods to Iraq. If he did not take offensive action, the president argued, Kuwait would be destroyed. The president's other advisers agreed. The time had come to get ready for war.

Powell disagreed with the president's decision, but, as a soldier, it was his duty to obey. If the president wanted an attack plan, Powell and his generals would devise the best plan they could.

"If there's going to be a war, if the American people know we have been committed to it, they will want it done quickly, decisively, and with as few casualties as possible," Powell remarked. "That's my job."

Immediately, the general began to increase the number of U.S. soldiers in Saudi Arabia. It would take more than 400,000 men and women to launch an offensive operation against Iraqi forces. Powell called on the American military commander in the Middle East, General H. Norman Schwarzkopf, to plan air and ground attacks. "I'm a great one for going to get help from people who know more than I," Powell said.

"Stormin' Norman" Schwarzkopf, a hefty man who stands 6 feet 3 inches tall, is an expert in military tactics. He understood that a war across the desert terrain would be difficult and dangerous. "I know what war is," said Schwarzkopf, who fought in Vietnam. "I am certainly anti-war. But I also believe there are things worth fighting for."

President Bush and the United Nations gave Saddam Hussein a deadline to withdraw his army

Powell and General H. Norman Schwarzkopf discuss combat plans at the airport in Riyadh, Saudi Arabia.

from Kuwait. He had until January 15, 1991. If he did not, his forces would be attacked.

Instead of withdrawing, though, Saddam Hussein spoke out bravely, bragging about his army's might. "Let everybody understand," he announced, "that this battle is going to become the mother of all battles."

Those words made it clear to Colin Powell that Saddam Hussein did not understand the strength of the American armed forces. "No Iraqi leader should think for a moment that we don't have the will or the ability to accomplish what might be required of us," Powell warned.

Powell believed that he knew how to defeat Iraq's army. His strategy was "very, very simple," he stated. "First, we're going to cut it off. And then we're going to kill it."

When Saddam Hussein ignored the U.N. deadline for withdrawal, President Bush chose the hour of attack. "H-hour" would be 3 AM, Saudi Arabian time, on January 17. Colin Powell waited at home with Alma, knowing he had done everything he could. While most Americans watched television news reports about the war, Colin and Alma Powell watched an old movie. "Without exception," Alma commented, "Colin is the calmest person I know."

In the early morning of January 17, Operation Desert Shield became Operation Desert Storm. From bases in Saudi Arabia, the first attack planes left the ground. The United States had taken a step from which it could not turn back.

Pilots from the United States and other nations dropped tens of thousands of bombs on Iraq. They

F-14A Tomcat aircraft fly over the desert during Operation Desert Storm.

destroyed the communication lines that linked Saddam Hussein and his troops. They blew up roads and bridges that carried supplies to Iraq's forces. The bombs destroyed military targets throughout Iraq and killed thousands of Iraqi soldiers.

The United States used several modern, "high-tech" weapons for the first time. Tomahawk missiles, launched from U.S. Navy warships, followed computerized maps to strike government buildings in Baghdad, the capital of Iraq. Americans watching television at home followed the paths of "smart bombs," weapons able to find their way to explode precisely on target.

The television audience got to know General Colin Powell as he reported to the nation on the war's progress. "Trust me," Powell said in one broadcast. His calm, confident manner earned that trust.

With the American people wanting a quick end to the war, Powell worked in his Pentagon office from dawn until dark.

"There were many long days and nights during the Gulf War," he said. "I talked with General Schwarzkopf several times each day. There were lots of meetings to discuss our plans and to evaluate how well our troops were doing. It was a very stressful time with constant concern for the men and women serving so bravely and so far from home."

His "Rules to Live By," posted on his desk, boosted Powell's confidence at difficult moments. "It can be done!" said one. "Have a vision. Be demanding," counseled another. A third rule com-

Powell became a familiar figure to Americans during numerous press briefings about the progress of the Persian Gulf War.

forted Powell at the end of a hectic, tiring day. "It ain't as bad as you think. It will look better in the morning," it said.

It surprised Powell and other military leaders that the Iraqis did little fighting back. They fired Scud missiles toward Saudi Arabia, but American Patriot anti-missiles exploded most of them before they hit the ground. Iraq also fired missiles at Israel, hoping to draw that nation into the war. But the Israelis refused to enter the fighting.

Saddam Hussein did wage a major assault on the environment. His forces dumped millions of gallons of oil into the Persian Gulf, creating the largest oil spill the world has ever seen. The oil killed marine life and polluted beaches. The Iraqis also set fire to oil wells, sending thick columns of smoke miles into the air. The smoke clouded the sky and dropped oily soot on the desert landscape.

After 38 days of air attacks, the ground war began. Since August, the Iraqi army had massed its strength along the border between Kuwait and Saudi Arabia. In a line stretching across Kuwait, they dug deep ditches designed to stop tanks. They built walls of sand and buried thousands of mines. Behind this fortified line, the Iraqis waited for the Americans and their allies to attack.

But General Schwarzkopf had no intention of attacking the Iraqi position head-on. He knew that he could save many lives by avoiding this fortified line. Under cover of night, the main attack force of American, Saudi, and British soldiers moved far to the west, beyond the end of the line.

At the same time, Schwarzkopf ordered ships carrying Marine units to anchor off Kuwait's coast, making it look as if the offensive would come from the east. As the Iraqis watched the coastline, the main strike force moved forward into Iraq, bypassing the fortified line, and then entered Kuwait from the west.

It took only four days of ground fighting before President Bush called for the shooting to stop. The war had been won. More than 100,000 Iraqis had been killed or wounded in the attack. American combat losses were 148 dead, 467 injured.

Even before the gunfire ended, masses of Iraqi soldiers surrendered to the Americans, relieved that their fight was over. One Iraqi soldier was shown kissing the hand of a U.S. Marine. And on February 27, 1991, Kuwaiti citizens welcomed the winning armies into Kuwait City.

"The city is ours again!" proclaimed the crowds of joyful Kuwaitis.

Powell speaks with an airman during the Persian Gulf War.

With the war over and Americans on their way home, a proud Colin Powell spoke to a group of people at the Vietnam Veterans Memorial in Washington. "What you've seen over and over is American troops bringing hope back to people who had none," General Colin Powell said. "And what a marvelous thing that is."

Chapter 8

Colin Powell Remembers

It was raining on April 15, 1991, as General Colin Powell approached his aunt's home. The few trees that grew along Union Avenue in the Bronx were starting to bud.

Military matters were far from Colin Powell's thoughts on this day. He had returned to Hunts Point, the Bronx neighborhood where he grew up. Powell knew that Hunts Point had changed since the 1950s. His boyhood home was now plagued by poverty, crime, and drugs.

The problem of drug use worries Colin Powell. "There's nothing America has to do of a higher priority to its security—national security and all kinds of security—than to get a handle on this drug problem," he says.

Colin Powell visited several sights in Hunts Point that reminded him of his childhood. He saw the apartment building on Kelly Street where he grew up. He rode past the White Castle restaurant where he shared hamburgers with his friends. As he looked around, Powell could not help but recall the images of his youth.

"I remember," Powell said, "I remember."

Powell also went back to Morris High School. He had been a student there 37 years earlier. The students gave him a plaque with a doorknob on it. The gift was meant to express the idea that education opens the door to opportunity. Standing before the students of Morris High, Powell talked about his own years at the school. "I remember the feeling that you can't make it," he said. "But you can."

Colin Powell understood the many problems that confronted the students assembled before him. And he knew that they often felt hopeless in the face of those problems. Many would drop out of high school before graduating. Powell urged them not to give up.

"If you get your diploma you are on your way somewhere," he told them. General Powell then gave the students an order. "I order you to stick with it," he commanded. "Get that diploma and stay off drugs."

Powell often speaks to America's young people. He has a special message for black youth. "Don't let your blackness, your minority status, be a problem to you," he tells young African Americans. "If you work hard, do the best you can, take advantage of every opportunity that's put in front of you, success will come your way."

"There's no substitute for hard work and study," Powell says. "People keep asking what is the secret to my success. There isn't any secret. I work hard. I spend long hours. I don't get distracted from the task before me. It's as simple as that."

In 1991, Colin Powell addresses students at his old high school.

73

In 1991, both Alma and Colin Powell received awards for their service to the United States.

Powell realizes that he learned how to be successful from his parents. "My heroes are my parents, Luther and Maud Powell," he says. "As I get older, I find I have a greater and greater appreciation for what my parents did for me. They set a wonderful example, demonstrating love and care and sacrifice for my sister and me as well as my many cousins."

"In their own quiet way," he continued, "they made it clear that there were certain expectations of each of us. That meant getting educated, getting a job, and going as far as you could with that job."

After the victory in the Gulf War, President Bush awarded Powell the Medal of Freedom, the nation's highest non-military award, for his work before and during the war. But the general was not the only Powell to receive awards.

On May 22, 1991, Alma Powell also received a medal. The U.S. Coast Guard presented her with its Distinguished Public Service Award for her years of volunteer work with the Red Cross.

Colin pinned the medal on Alma's dress. "You see the way she stood at attention? I taught her that," he joked.

Powell traveled to Detroit in August 1991 to honor the Tuskegee Airmen, the black World War II pilots whose accomplishments helped to improve opportunities for other African Americans. "I am here because of you," Powell told the pilots.

Colin Powell takes great pride in the tradition of African-American military service. "No group of Americans ever served this nation with greater devotion, greater loyalty, greater sacrifice, than African Americans," he says.

It is a tradition of service that includes the black soldiers who have fought in every American war, a tradition of sacrifice that includes Crispus Attucks, the Buffalo Soldiers, and Benjamin Davis, Jr. It is a tradition that now includes Colin Powell.

Some people have wondered whether Colin Powell might one day be vice president or even president of the United States. Powell dismisses the idea for now.

In 1991, President Bush appointed Powell to a second two-year term as chairman of the Joint Chiefs of Staff. The appointment was confirmed by the U.S. Senate later that year.

"What I have always loved to do is serve in the Army," General Colin Powell says. "What I have always wanted to do is the very best I can."

Chronology:
African Americans in the U.S. Armed Forces

1770	On March 5, Crispus Attucks, a former slave, is among the first to die in the "Boston Massacre."
1776-1781	7,000 African-American soldiers and sailors take part in the Revolutionary War.
1776	On January 16, the Continental Congress agrees to enlist free blacks.
1812-1815	Black soldiers and sailors fight against British troops at such critical battles as Lake Erie and New Orleans.
1862-1865	186,000 African-American soldiers serve in black regiments during the Civil War; 38,000 black soldiers lose their lives in more than 400 battles.
1862	On July 17, the U.S. Congress approves the enlistment of black soldiers.
1865	On March 13, the Confederate States of America begins to accept black recruits.
1866-1890	Units of black soldiers, referred to as Buffalo Soldiers, are formed as part of the U.S. Army.
1872	On September 21, John H. Conyers becomes the first African American admitted to the U.S. Naval Academy.
1877	On June 15, Henry O. Flipper becomes the first African American to graduate from West Point.
1914-1918	More than 400,000 African Americans serve in the U.S. armed forces during the First World War.

On May 15, two black soldiers, Henry Johnson and Needham Roberts become the first Americans to receive the French Medal of Honor (*Croix de Guerre*).	1918
In June, Benjamin O. Davis, Jr., graduates from West Point, the first black American to do so in the twentieth century.	1936
Benjamin O. Davis, Sr., becomes the first African-American general in the active Regular Army.	1940
American forces in World War II include more than a million African-American men and women.	1941-1945
On March 25, the Army Air Corps forms its first black unit, the 99th Pursuit Squadron.	1941
On August 24, Colonel Benjamin O. Davis, Jr., is made commander of the 99th Pursuit Squadron.	1942
On January 27 and 28, the airmen of the 99th Pursuit Squadron score a major victory against enemy fighters at the Italian seaside town of Anzio.	1944
On February 2, President Harry S Truman signs Executive Order 9981, ordering an end to segregation in the U.S. armed forces.	1948
Black and white forces fight side by side in Korea as separate black fighting units are disbanded.	1950-1953
Twenty African-American soldiers are awarded the Congressional Medal of Honor during the Vietnam War.	1965-1973
On April 28, Samuel L. Gravely becomes the first black admiral in the history of the U.S. Navy.	1971
In August, Daniel "Chappie" James becomes the first African American to achieve the rank of four-star general.	1975
On October 3, Colin Powell becomes the first African-American chairman of the Joint Chiefs of Staff.	1989
100,000 African-American men and women are sent to the Middle East during the Persian Gulf conflict.	1990-1991

Index

Bibliography

Adelman, Ken. "Ground Zero: Colin Powell on War, Peace, and Balancing at the Center of Power." *Washingtonian,* May 1990.

Cannon, Lou. "Antidote to Ollie North." *The Washington Post Magazine,* August 7, 1988.

Potts, Paula Lee. "A Conversation With Alma Powell." *Military Lifestyle,* May 1990.

Powell, Colin L. Letter to the author, August 19, 1991.

Randolph, Laura B. "General Colin L. Powell: The World's Most Powerful Soldier." *Ebony,* February 1990.

Rowan, Carl T. "Called to Service: The Colin Powell Story." *Reader's Digest,* December 1989.

Trescott, Jacqueline. "General Colin Powell's Buddy System." *The Washington Post,* February 25, 1991.

Wakin, Edward. *Black Fighting Men in U.S. History.* New York: Lothrop, Lee & Shepherd, 1971.

Waskow, Arthur I. *From Race Riot to Sit-In: 1919 and the 1960s.* Garden City, NY: Doubleday, 1966.

Weinberger, Caspar W. "General Colin Powell—An Inside View." *Forbes,* January 22, 1990.

Wolff, Craig. "General Powell Sees the Bronx He Loved, In Memory." *The New York Times,* April 16, 1991.

Woodward, Bob. *The Commanders.* New York: Simon & Schuster, 1991.